# CREATING BUSINESS SUCCESS WITH FACEBOOK - THE EASY WAY!

## ALUN HILL

*I think a simple rule of business is, if you do the things that are easier first, then you can actually make a lot of progress.*

— MARK ZUCKERBERG

# CONTENTS

## PART THREE

# PREFACE

Mark Zuckerberg launched Facebook from his Harvard University dormitory room on February 4, 2004.

He was assisted by his college roommates and fellow Harvard students Eduardo Saverin, Andrew McCollum, Dustin Moskovitz, and Chris Hughes.

Since 2010, *Time* magazine has named Zuckerberg among the 100 wealthiest and most influential people in the world as a part of its Person of the Year award.

In December 2016, Zuckerberg was ranked 10th on the Forbes list of The World's Most Powerful People.

Alun Hill, your author, has studied Facebook intensively since its inception and used it to successfully build many of his 32 businesses.

Today, **Creating Business Success With Facebook** is easy .. if you follow carefully the steps in this book.

---

*Alun Hill, Malta, 2017*

# PART ONE

# Chapter One

# CREATING BUSINESS SUCCESS WITH FACEBOOK - THE EASY WAY!

IT USED TO BE THAT PEOPLE WOULD SIT AND FIGURE OUT HOW TO make Facebook posts most appealing to Facebook's algorithms.

If that's you, forget that strategy - it no longer applies. Without advertising, a limited number of people will see your posts, and this is especially true for Facebook Pages.

But there's a third alternative that many people don't notice or pay attention to: Creating engaging posts that actually get shared.

Your Facebook success is all in the sharing. You can have six people viewing a post, but if one of those people has a larger audience and shares your post, it is suddenly exposed to your sharer's entire audience.

If members of that sharer's audience share your post, your audience then increases by their audiences. And all that can happen rapidly, in what will seem like the blink of an eye—providing you've created a post that people find irresistible to share.

In this book, I'm going to get in touch with the reality of Facebook today, and show you how to free yourself of the headache of laboriously planning your post content for SEO—while generating endless ideas for coming up with engaging posts that actually get shared.

Let's start by looking at what Facebook likes—and what it doesn't.

You can mix your media in Facebook—text, images, infographics and videos. Facebook also is strongly receptive to posts with personality and a unique voice—which means it is also unreceptive to posts that read like slick advertisements (unless you have actually created an ad!) Keep the promotional posts to ads.

That being said...

**Step One: Advertise**

Today's Facebook is largely geared towards those who advertise. No matter how great your posts are, their reach will be very limited if you don't invest even a small amount in advertising—and it's easy to do. Watch your posts, and see which ones get the most engagement in views, likes and shares.

It's easy to boost your **best-performing posts** by clicking the "Boost" button, when you're on your Facebook Page.

However, take the time to check your posts in your Facebook Insights. That's where you'll not only get an overview of all your posts (and how well they stack up against each other) but how many likes and shares they've received too, in graphic format.

B e sure to learn about Facebook Ads and specify a custom audience for your ads. Without that step, your ad will be served up to a random audience; many of whom will be poor quality contacts.

Facebook Advertising is an absolute "must" if you are looking for maximum reach in a short period of time—for fast lead generation—but the best way to get your content to the right people organically is to make sure you post content that people love to share. (That's what the rest of the book is going to cover.)

**Step Two: Post Updates on Your Facebook Page**

Don't be afraid to post business updates on your Facebook Page —and ask people to share them.

Yes, Facebook would rather you keep these as paid ads—but people often skip paid ads, as a matter of course. But think about it, fans have followed you because they like your business or you, as a coach. They like what you're branding. So share what's going on— that's entirely possible, without being spammy.

**Step Three: Keep it Current**

Facebook likes posts that discuss **hot topics**. Remember that Facebook Pages are public, so if you talk about topics currently trending like wildfire, your chances of having that post appear to more people increase (but remember to **keep it relevant to your brand** too!)

The drawback? Your voice is likely to get drowned out in a sea of other voices all shouting about the same thing—so increase your odds by:

- Including a powerful graphic
- Using both popular and unique, specific keywords
- Including a Call to Action at the end or a strong incentive to share

**Step Four: Maximize Your Posts**

When you write a post for Facebook, customize it and share it on other platforms too. Just keep in mind the different reasons people use each different platform—then ask people to share on those specific platforms too:

- **Slideshare**—If your post can be broken down into even three or four points, you can expand it into a Slideshare post. Use your keywords and think of Slideshare as a high-powered amplifier for your Facebook and blog posts
- **Pinterest**—people are looking for information and ideas before they buy

- **Twitter**—If you've created a powerful hashtag and have at least one lead generation keyword, repurpose your post in short form on Twitter. (Leave room for responses.)
- **LinkedIn**—LinkedIn is where people go for serious networking, checking out profiles (e.g. yours) and information. And since the addition of LinkedIn Pulse on mobile, double your post power by creating for Facebook and LinkedIn regularly
- **Facebook**—According to Facebook itself, its most popular posts—surpassing even those on currently trending topics such as Donald Trump—are "links about lifestyle hacks, celebrities, friendship and parenting". (If you are a lifestyle coach, this is good news for you!)

If you create your post and adapt versions instantly for your audience's key networks, it is not that much extra work: You write one main post and with a little tweaking, you gain maximum social networking reach. (The same goes for graphics—keep raw, immediate snaps for Instagram and gorgeous, professional shots for Facebook and Pinterest.)

**Step Five: Plan Your Posts**

Most people have a thought, type it into Facebook and hit "Post". How many times have you done this then re-read it and found an embarrassing typo? Or realized that you missed writing a crucial sentence—one that makes the rest of the post clear?

If you are using posts for branding or lead generation, by all means come up with spontaneous thoughts and ideas to post—but then STOP. Plan your post. Write it in Notepad before ever posting it to Facebook.

Here's how to do it:

- **Decide what your main point is**. If you have more than one point, split them into separate posts.
- **Write your post** (still in Notepad or whatever text editor you like to use).
- **Do something else for a while**—finish reading your feed or Page, make notes, go check your email.
- **Re-read your new post**. With a little distance between when you first thought it up and what you're re-reading now, it will be easier to spot grammatical errors, sentences that don't quite make sense, spelling mistakes and information you missed including.

- **Go through your post again**. Take out weak words like adjectives and adverbs; and unnecessary words. Make sure your post is as short as you can make it.
- **Add a Graphic**. This instantly boost your share-ability level in Facebook's eyes.
- **Press "Post"**.

**Step Six: Create and Use Powerful Hashtags**

Yes, hashtags work on Facebook as well as Twitter. You can search them. And each hashtag will have its own unique URL.

Popular hashtags can increase your Facebook post reach—but don't use more than two, tops; otherwise it may have the reverse effect and kill your post.

Find hashtags that are already potent by visiting Hashtags.org and checking out:

- Trending Hashtags
- Popular Hashtags

Pay particular attention to what is trending *on Facebook*, however: And use hashtags associated with those trends.

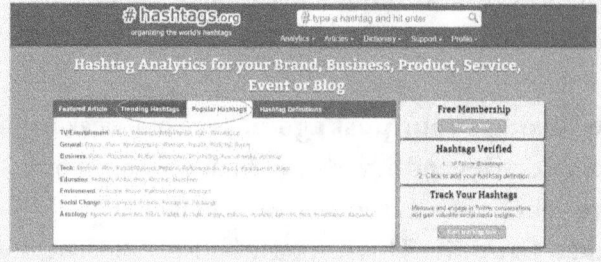

## Step Seven: Avoiding the Post Killers

Just as there are best post-types on Facebook, there are also Facebook posts that will do damage; ranging from ones that simply get ignored by all and sundry (including Facebook) right up to ones that will get you banned and unfriended in the same instance.

**Bad graphics**: Most of us know not to post incredibly graphic images of torture, violence or horrific injuries (yet I actually unfriended a person this morning for doing just that. I am still recovering from the unthinkably horrific image, and it was a tremendous shock to see it.)

Why do people post content like this? Some of our most well-meaning friends do it from social conscience, and have the purest of motives—but no one should inflict graphic horrors without warning. Even if they're not as unbearable as the one I just saw, constantly posting notices about animal cruelty or similar subjects is a way not only to drive away your friends and fans, but also trigger Facebook to start limiting your post visibility.

**Negative posts**: Do you post content that makes people hide your posts? Big on this list of Facebook no-no's is:

- Continual complaining
- Obsessive or irrelevant posts
- "Venting"

You need to keep all your posts relevant to your audience. Don't post endless knitting patterns if your prime audience is equally obsessively into computer technology. And if every post is complaining in tone, people will start hiding them. And "venting" is a luxury you can't afford, if you're running a Facebook business Page —unless your "vent" is highly relevant to your audience and you're actually venting on their behalf.

**Empty posts:** Do you post for the sake of posting? If you catch yourself doing this—don't! People will soon skip your posts— or worse, hide them—if you rattle off too many "inspirational" quotes or cute kitten photos in a day. And multiple baby pictures are best kept for grandparents.

**Too many graphics uploaded at once:** Another

phenomenon that often results in people skipping your posts: Posting more than four graphics at once, tops. (How many times have you seen "9+" in the corner of a batch of photos—and either skipped them or just clicked "Like" instead of looking through each individual photo?)

If a photo is not important *to your reader*, don't post it.

**Spammy or promotional posts**: Facebook most likely cares about spammy posts more than they do about other types. If you are going to do any sort of promotion, they want you to take out an ad—and even then, if you promote something across more than one Facebook Group, prepare to be banned from Facebook!

Rule of thumb: Keep promotion for ads—or keep it conversational and real.

### *On your personal feed*:

**Okay**: "My new book, "Pot Gardening", is finally out! It's about gardening in containers. It's being released on Amazon today." [photograph of book cover]

**Not okay**: "Are you looking for a solution to bending over in the garden and wrecking your back? Nerys Nermal's new book, "Pot Gardening" will make you rethink your plan of retiring from the garden! Go buy it today! [link]

### *On your Facebook Page*:

Product announcements are acceptable, if you keep them highly personalized and avoid sounding like an ad you're not paying for.

**Duplicate product announcements in multiple Facebook Groups**: This one will get you banned from those Groups quicker than you can blink—even if the Group is your own.

**Step Eight: Verify Your Facebook Page**

If you have a "publicly listed" phone number for your business, you can—and should—verify your Facebook Page.

What that does is allow you to use a new feature: **Facebook Live**.

Here's how to verify your Page:

- Go to **Settings>>General>>Page Verification>>Verify Page>>Get Started**
- Enter your phone number
- Select **Call Me Now**

Facebook will call you back to verify your Page.

What you need to know about Facebook Live: It is supposed to be available to all Pages at this time, but Facebook is still introducing the feature slowly, attempting to control bandwidth. For this reason, they are looking for Pages with quality content and quality live-streaming feeds.

Even you don't want to (or can't) use Facebook Live, remember that you can still upload your own videos to your Facebook feeds.

## Step Nine: Questions and Polls

One of the best ways to engage people with your posts is by making the post ask a question.

You would think that simply asking your question would be good enough, but it's usually not. There are some tricks to turning this around, however:

- **Use a poll** like https://www.facebook.com/OpinionPolls/

Simply click on the **Use App** button to create your poll.

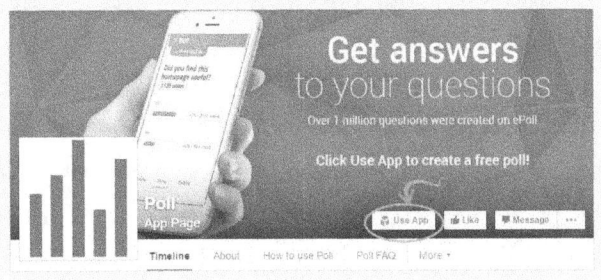

N ote that you can add videos, images and styles to your Poll. You can also choose to allow respondents to share their opinions.

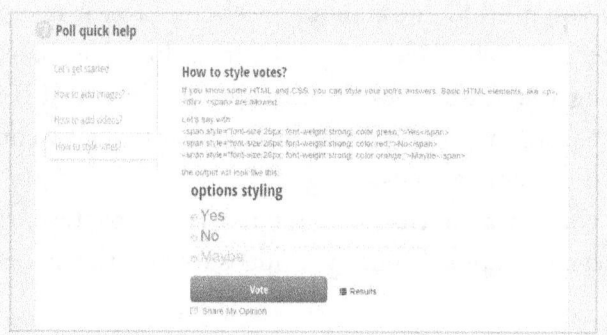

The Opinions poll is the easiest app to use on Facebook—and by providing people with options and promising immediacy, your poll post can be very appealing.

Notice that you can also choose to:

- Send to friends and fans
- Set up a campaign (paid option)

Be sure to customize your poll response button and preview your poll. (You will be able to edit it.)

You can also vary your post content by creating quizzes and "personality tests" too.

- **Give them a choice**: We've already seen an example of this principle with the Opinions app. Don't ask "What's your favorite color?": Instead, personalize your question and give them a choice.

Example:

**Low rate of response:**

**High rate of response**

What's your favorite color?

If you could be a color, which one would you be?

- Red
- Blue
- Green

Give choices in your regular posts, when asking a question.

- **Ask a question on a hot topic**: Choose a topic where opinions are already flying back and forth
- **Ask questions in your Facebook Groups**, as well as in your Facebook Page

### Step Ten: Keep it Short!

We've spoken about planning your Facebook posts—and also about editing. This will help you do something else that is crucial to capturing shares and attention: Keep your posts short. A study by BuddyMedia reported that posts of 80 characters or less have 27% higher engagement rates. (Think in terms of one post line equalling 60 characters.)

Keeping it short means getting your point across with impact! Note the number of views (1.2m) and the number of shares on this post (899).

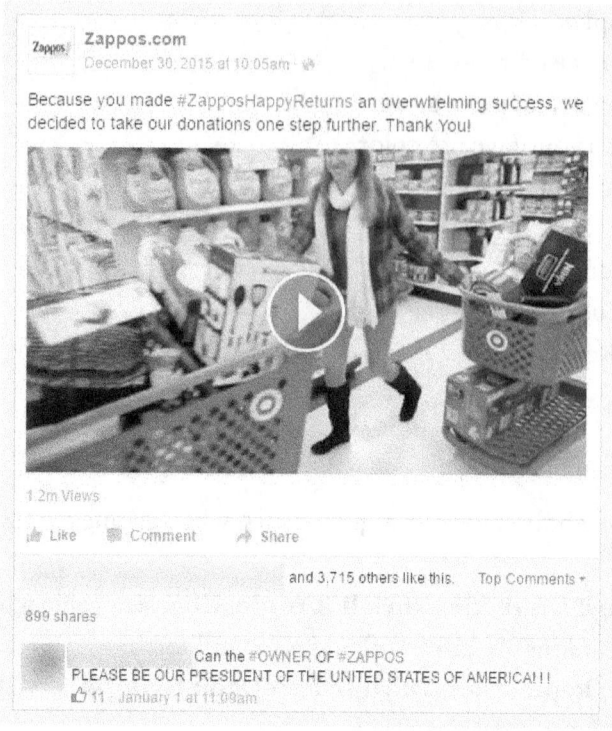

Zappos.com just posted a simple "Thank You"—but the video accompanying it aroused curiosity and promised a "feel good" moment.

A word of warning: Keeping posts short *does not* mean making cryptic statements.

I n fact, cryptic personal statements not only devalue your personal or page Facebook feed; they devalue it in Facebook's eyes. Too many of these self-indulgent comments will reduce your reach.

Here's a perfect example of a short post with high incentive to click (for the right audience):

## Step Eleven: Make People Curious

While using calls to action (CTAs) is a tried-and-true marketing strategy, there is division among top experts and Facebook authority sites on how effective it is for Facebook.

- Some argue that CTAs such as "Like" or "Share" reduce reach.
- Others argue that it expands viral buzz.

Your best bet is to simply avoid the whole issue by **making people curious**—as Zappos.com did so effectively in our previous example. Give them something to click through to—and then **pitch your CTA on the new page or site**.

(If you want to gather more Facebook "Likes", create a Facebook ad specifically for that purpose—and be sure to choose a **custom audience** that reflects your ideal client.)

Use post titles, headlines, questions and photos to rouse curiosity in your ideal audience and your ideal client.

Finally, do your best to allow the curiosity/entertainment factor to generate spontaneous shares, rather than relying solely on CTAs.

**Step Twelve: Encourage Customer Service Posts Directly On Your Facebook Page**

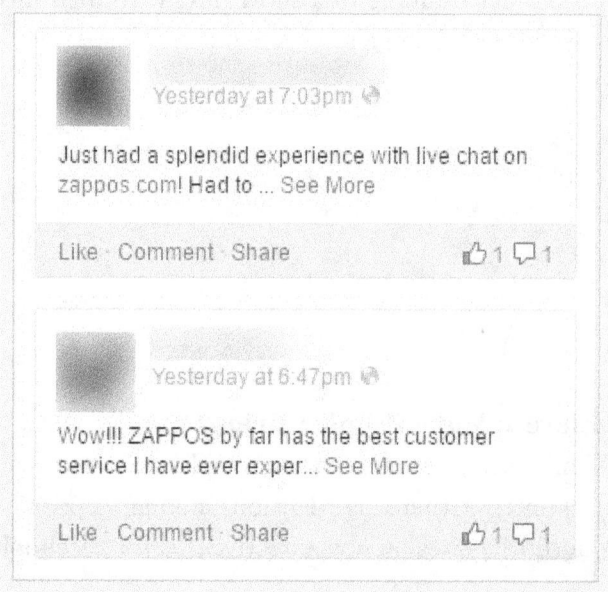

Again, let's look to Zappos.com as a perfect example. These are the sort of comments you will always see under Visitor Posts, in the left margin of the company's page.

Answering questions immediately shows your fans that you are there and that you care.

It shows your values and your efficiency too, as well as building trust.

But you have to make sure you take care of customer service posts within 24 hours.

**Step Thirteen: Make Sure Your Links Are Worth Clicking On!**

There have been many complaints that it is no longer so easy to figure out what Facebook wants/what works on Facebook, these days—but Facebook itself provides the answers, if you make a point of checking in daily at Facebook Newsroom.

[PRESENTER: https://newsroom.fb.com/news/]

For example, in a newsroom article on click baiting (something you or I would never do), Facebook states: "If people click on an article and spend time reading it, it suggests they clicked through to something valuable. If they click through to a link and then come straight back to Facebook, it suggests that they didn't find something that they wanted. With this update we will start taking into account whether people tend to spend time away from Facebook after clicking a link, or whether they tend to come straight back to News Feed when we rank stories with links in them."

The article also reveals that Facebook looks at the ratio of people clicking on the content, comparing the clicks to whether or not the viewers discuss and share these links with their friends.

Specifically, they are talking about posts with clickable headlines, graphics and videos here. For links within text posts, Facebook prefers including the link above any accompanying photographs, rather than making the photo itself the link. Facebook concludes: "With this update, we will prioritize showing links in the link-format, and show fewer links shared in captions or status updates."

(If you're confused about what exactly this means, simply **paste your link while drafting your post**.)

**Step Fourteen: Suit Your Post Media to Your Story Type and Audience**

You've no doubt been told hundreds of times to mix your post media types. This is all well and good, but it's more important to make sure the media type you use most is the best one for your audience and their viewing preferences—as well as for your story.

For example, if you want to teach your viewers how to use software, video is usually the best type of media. If you want them to help you celebrate a victory, show them the moment of achievement—and keep it relevant. (Example: You are a show jumping coach, and your six-year-old just won her first class. While parental boasting is usually high on the list of what bores an audience, the topic—winning a jump class—would be relevant to this particular audience; plus, you would personalize the pride you feel in your daughter, which transfers to your clients and followers.)

If you're a writer, make sure a good proportion of your posts are text posts. Yes, still use killer graphics—but make sure they don't overshadow what you have to say in print.

If your audience are fans of your podcasts, share links to audio files—and make sure your cover photo includes a sign-up tab, so they catch every new episode.

When telling your story, use the well-known story-telling principle of "show; don't tell". This isn't as rigid a guideline as "use a photo". What it really means is "engage your viewers' emotions. Put them in the saddle. Let them feel the wind, taste the rain, smell the forest".

It's up to you to decide which medium will accomplish this task best for each post.

**Step Fifteen: Anticipate**

Remember that computing and digital communication are always about the future. Things change even while you're getting used to "new" changes. Checking out sites like Facebook's newsroom (especially the Q & A with Mark section) for big clues.

Some examples:

- Facebook is already using artificial intelligence (AI) to help with areas like accessibility and mobile usage
- Facebook is devoting more attention to mobile profiles, developing such features as a **video profile photo**
- Facebook's primary focus in post monitoring is posts that get shared (yet they don't like you to ask for a share. They want it to be viral and organic)

Building into your schedule even five minutes of daily Facebook research (for example, reading authority sites and blogs) can help you come up with posts that gain maximum attention, Facebook approval and reach.

**Step Sixteen: Don't Shorten Links on Facebook**

Again, let's turn to BuddyMedia. In the study previously mentioned, this social media optimization organization also discovered that posts got less shares when URL shorteners were used.

In a recent Slideshare presentation, they report that **engagement rates were three times higher** when posts included "a full URL".

**Step Seventeen: Pay Attention to Optimum Post Time**

It's become almost a tradition to do most of our Facebook posting during business hours. However, BuddyMedia notes 20% more engagement when posts are created after 4 p.m.

That being said, the best time to post is always when your particular audience is online... And you also have to take into account where the most active percentage of your audience lies: Is it in a different time zone? The other side of the world? Are they people who only post from work? Who only post after hours? Are your posts retail based? If so, try posting after work hours!

A policy of Facebook awareness is best. Check your Page post overviews in Facebook Insights. Look through your previous day's posts every day, and see when you had the highest engagement.

Do this consistently for more than a couple of days, to get a real feel for true fan patterns and habits.

**Step Eighteen: Optimize Your Facebook Page for Mobile**

Be sure to check out the Public View of your Facebook feeds on your mobile device. This is what a major percentage of your audience will be seeing. How can you improve what they see? How do your competitors' feeds differ from yours? Are there any tips you can pick up from your competitors' mobile-optimized feeds?

Meanwhile, keep these tips in mind:

- Remember that you can drag photos and drop (reposition) them, when "telling a story" with more than one photo, if you're using your mobile

- Keep your mobile-targeted photos to a dimension of 560 x 292 pixels
- Remember that the maximum number of characters ideally seen on a mobile screen without scrolling is 120-150 characters—up to 480 characters less than on a PC screen
- Make sure your first line is the most engaging/most important
- Be aware that the number of characters allowed/seen in mobile offers equals those seen in a PC screen: 25-90 characters

**Step Nineteen: Know Your Facebook Images**

You can increase both reach and engagement by knowing everything there is to know about what works best, when posting images to Facebook:

1. **Familiarize yourself with optimum sizes** for each different type of Facebook image. The ultimate guide is currently Jon Loomer's Facebook Image Dimensions Infographic, which has every size for every type of Facebook image listed in one handy sheet.

[PRESENTER: http://www.jonloomer.com/facebook-image-dimensions-infographic-pdf/]

1. **Keep personal photos for your feed**; relevant, high-quality ones for your Page. (The exception would be if

you are showing a personal angle to your company—for example, a Christmas photo of your employees on a company sleigh ride.)

2. **Create a catchy headline or title for your photo**. This will be your hook! Intrigue them, or prompt them to answer.

3. **Create an Image Folder before posting to Facebook.** Always be on the lookout for top quality professional photos that fit your business topic and signature theme. Pick them up before you need them, and re-name the photos with relevant keywords. This will save you much time when you are hunting around for images.

Use only reputable stock sites (free or paid) and do check the licenses. (For example, does the site/license allow commercial use? If a person's face was featured, do they include a model release?) A negative to either of these last two questions is a big, red flag to stay away from that image or site.

The best strategy: Hire your own photographer. Outsource your photos for truly original images—or take up photography and provide you own.

**Step Twenty: Know Your Audience!**

TIP: Visualize your best client, when creating posts for your Facebook Page—or a particular person you'd like to reach.

This doesn't just involve being observant on which posts engage, it also involves correctly targeting your audience in the first place—and never forgetting who you are talking to.

To find your ideal client:

- **Focus on your coaching's most life-changing benefit or change** that clients experience
- **Calculate what you need to make this year**
- **Calculate what your ideal client is willing to pay**

**for and can afford**. Do you need to attract a higher income bracket? Does this client prefer single events or packages?

- **Check your assets**—then see what you can add. Do you need to write a book? Retire money-losing offers; or ones that attract a lower income bracket than you want to work with? Offer (and post about) a time-limited close-out special.
- Offer a special package? Create VIP Events. Take time to set these changes in motion first—and you will really have something to post about!
- **Find out what other online services, apps and software potential clients use**. Are they heavy software users? Outsourcers? Self-help webinar enthusiasts? Anything that tips you off to common ideal client behaviors will help you in your targeting.

(These will also tip you off to the right keywords to include in post titles, headlines, hashtags and posts.)

- **Check your feedback**. Remember to include feedback forms with in-person events, on your website, after strategy sessions and in books and other PDFs. Ask questions and create polls for your Facebook Groups and Pages. Create custom audiences and dark posts for your Facebook ads—as well as A/B split tests.

Pay attention to the results!

**Step Twenty-One: Create a Closed Facebook Group for Better Post Content**

If you have even half a dozen clients, there is no excuse for not creating a closed or secret Facebook Group, and engaging with them there.

The reason? People tend to be a lot more responsive in closed or secret groups—particularly if they are exclusive, and feel like an "inner circle".

If active and run intelligently, a Facebook Group will trigger:

- More honest reactions to posts
- Complaints (hopefully only occasional ones! But don't shy away from complaints: They give you a chance to demonstrate your exceptional customer service and/or ability to really listen.)
- More focused questions
- Honest feedback
- Suggestions
- Higher engagement
- Better quality responses
- More relevant member posts
- Tips and other valuable links

And what is more important, you will be **building trust** with your group members—and you will be able to observe how they interact with each other. What personal comments they make and what personal problems escape. (This is what happens in a **community**—which is what good Facebook Groups become.) You'll see how they deal with issues; hear what is bothering them and be able to identify pain points—and future packages or products.

No, you won't expand your reach hugely with a Group—but you will generate authority status (particularly if you interact daily and post links to new resources and articles) and get to know your ideal audience even better.

And **this knowledge can carry over to your Facebook Page posts**. (Think of running a Facebook Group as an investment!)

All these suggestions can help you improve the quality of your Facebook posts—but do remember to, first and foremost, be authentic and speak with your own honest, unique voice.

# PART TWO

*Chapter Two*

# 21 WAYS TO FACEBOOK SUCCESS

HERE ARE TWENTY-ONE WAYS TO ENSURE THAT YOUR FACEBOOK posts engage more people.

*Chapter One*

# MAKE YOUR FACEBOOK ADS FEEL PERSONAL AND CONVERSATIONAL

Client case studies show that ads feeling like a normal part of your fan's feed—like posts—have a noticeably higher conversion and click-through rate than ads that are obviously advertisements.

(Notice the difference between the comments, Likes and shares between these two ads.

The first ad is a conversational post from Steve Harrison; the second a traditional ad from Infusionsoft.

Jack Canfield—the subject of Harrison's ad—and Infusionsoft have relatively equal visibility and authority: Yet Harrison's conversational-post-style add gathers a stunningly higher number of comments, Likes and shares.)

*Chapter Two*

# FOCUS ON YOUR FANS

WHEN WE POST ON OUR FACEBOOK FEEDS, IT IS NATURAL TO first think of what we need to say—that's why there are so many self-indulgent, cryptic or "empty" posts.

Before you ever log onto Facebook (or any other social media platform) think about your ideal client. What is she interested in?

What would help her, interest her or entertain her?

Get into the habit of focusing on your ideal client before posting, and you will soon see your engagement rate rise.

# Chapter Three

# DON'T BE AFRAID TO POST THE OCCASIONAL BIT OF PURE FUN

Something that genuinely makes your audience laugh is always a hit—and it needn't spoil your branding, if you pick your subject carefully.

(For example, the photo above would be perfect if you know that a high percentage of your clients have cats, and post about them regularly.)

*Chapter Four*

# MAKE SURE YOUR BOOSTED POSTS ARE ALWAYS RELEVANT

For example, if a post was related to a particular holiday, remember to stop the post once the holiday is over!

And don't boost popular posts if their timeliness and relevance is past, no matter how many shares they got.

*Chapter Five*

# POST ALL THE TIME

THERE'S REALLY NO WAY AROUND IT, YOU HAVE TO POST consistently in order to keep people—and Facebook—engaged with your feeds.

Creating a post plan and logging into content idea/scheduling sites like Post Planner or CoSchedule will help you keep on top of this in minimal time per day.

# Chapter Six

# EXPLORE CURATED CONTENT 1. EXPLORE CURATED CONTENT

In addition to rotating your post media types, explore sharing other people's relevant content.

A mix of your own posts and curated content seems to work best on Facebook, according to Facebook expert, Mari Smith.

Just make sure you introduce your curated content with why you are sharing it (why your ideal reader will care).

*Chapter Seven*

## CONSIDER FACEBOOK DARK POSTS

IF YOU DON'T KNOW WHAT A "DARK POST" IS, REMEDY THAT—fast—by reading Facebook Dark Posts: What They Are and Why Use them.

http://www.marismith.com/facebook-dark-posts-what-are-they-and-why-use-them/

# Chapter Eight

# ACQUAINT YOURSELF WITH CUSTOM AUDIENCES

You've heard it's important to use custom audiences in your Facebook sponsored posts, but that involves more than just selecting a few keywords.

Read this article from State of Digital on fifteen specific ways to use the custom audience feature to the max.

http://www.stateofdigital.com/15-ways-to-use-facebook-custom-audiences/

*Chapter Nine*

# FIND ROUTINES TO MAKE POSTING EXCITING

IF YOU FEEL YOU "HAVE" TO POST EVERY DAY, IT WILL SOON become a chore. That's why it's important to find and create routines to keep posting fun and exciting for you, as well as your fans.

One quick way to do this: Take a day every week to brainstorm post ideas. Do this on a day that is separate from post writing.

Then, when you need an idea, just reference wherever you store ideas.

(You can even post them on colorful sticky notes and do a random "eyes-shut" selection.)

Not only will routines like these stimulate your creativity, they will help you write better posts!

*Chapter Ten*

# THINK ABOUT THE SPECIFIC GOAL FOR EACH FACEBOOK VIDEO

ONE THING YOU'LL OFTEN SEE ON FACEBOOK, WHEN IT COMES TO videos: People making the same type of video, over and over.

Don't do that—it's the quickest way to get people to tune-out-and-skip.

Think about what you want your Facebook video to achieve before making it—and realize you can tailor videos to all sorts of goals, including:

- Teaching
- Demonstrating
- Entertaining
- Giving shout-outs and recognition to your clients/fans
- Inspiring and uplifting
- Show a milestone moment actually occurring (one that will be important to your viewer)
- Showing what's possible
- Giving a tour of your location

*Chapter Eleven*

# FIND OUT WHEN YOUR IDEAL FANS ARE ONLINE

WHAT REALLY WORKS WELL WITH BUILDING TRUST AND engaging people on Facebook:

Responding to a comment or post while they are actually online.

Ditto, posting your own posts—that's when someone comments, and you answer.

(The easiest way to do this? Check your Facebook Page Insights.)

*Chapter Twelve*

# ANALYZE YOUR SUCCESS

REMEMBERING THAT ONLY 90 CHARACTERS ARE RECOMMENDED for mobile Facebook viewing, play with different post lengths.

See what common denominators your most successful posts share.

- Do they have photographs? No photograph? Links? Videos?
- Are they longer or shorter posts?
- Are they posted at a different time of day?
- Were they timely and relevant?
- What type of post were they? Informational, funny, breaking-news, inspirational, quote, tip, infographic and so forth

*Chapter Thirteen*

# BE THERE TO CARE

WE ARE STILL VERY MUCH IN THE AGE OF HEART-FELT marketing, so make sure that when you're on Facebook, you put helping and caring about your fans highest on the list.

Even if your particular fans are not an emotional bunch, identify with their interests, help them beat their biggest challenges and walk every step of the way with them towards their biggest goals.

# Chapter Fourteen

# GIVE THEM SOMETHING TO DO—THEN MAKE THEM WANT TO DO IT

DON'T JUST GO FOR PASSIVE "LIKES". GIVING YOUR FACEBOOK followers something to do—prompting them to take action—is what hooks and engages them with you.

Make sure that action is clearly spelled out, and stands alone—don't ask them to do five things.

Point out the big benefit of doing it immediately—even if it's simply that they will lose out if they don't.

(Example: "Fifty Ways to Make Your Workspace More Efficient" is free only for today on Amazon. Pick it up while you can—there's about six hours left.")

*Chapter Fifteen*

# BE PERSONAL

IT'S ONE THING TO MAKE SURE YOUR POSTS ARE RELEVANT AND helpful—but don't be afraid to let your unique personality show through. It is what makes the wrong audience run away—and the right one enthusiastically follow and engage.

*Chapter Sixteen*

# CREATE A THEME

NOT A MEME—THOSE HAVE ACTUALLY FALLEN OUT OF FAVOR WITH Facebook.

But do something distinctive with your posts that only you do.

For example, one coach creates inspirational nature photographs with hand-written captions, heavily loaded with imagery (she's a spiritual coach) and painted in Japanese pen and ink.

A particular artist always posts fractal drawings with glowing colors—instantly recognizable.

Another coach has her dog present "Millie's Monday" posts—all with a message that resonates with her clients.

Themed posts are a great way to instantly brand yourself for recognition.

*Chapter Seventeen*

# PLAN FOR FACEBOOK LIVE

EVEN IF YOU DON'T YET HAVE ACCESS TO FACEBOOK LIVE, PLAN for it, if you're interested in live broadcasting via Facebook.

Check out articles like this one on Social Media Examiner (and follow Social Media Examiner for up-to-date breaking Facebook news).

http://www.socialmediaexaminer.com/facebook-live-what-marketers-need-to-know/

# Chapter Eighteen

# THROW OCCASIONAL CONTESTS INTO YOUR FACEBOOK POST MIX

USE APPS LIKE SHORTSTACK OR WOOBOX TO EASILY CREATE contests your fans will like.

Make the prize either something frivolously fun or something incredibly helpful—a set of your templates, for example.

Just make sure your contests follow Facebook's guidelines.

https://www.facebook.com/page_guidelines.php#promotionsguidelines

*Chapter Nineteen*

## TELL A STORY

DON'T JUST SHARE A LINK—INCLUDE EVEN A ONE-SENTENCE anecdote to personalize it to your viewer and you.

Don't just post a photo—evoke a feeling, and emotion. Remind your fans of their own similar stories with your photo.

- Share a failure; then offer hope.
- Make a promise; then keep it.
- Be real.

*Chapter Twenty*

# MAKE A PROMISE IN THE FIRST SENTENCE

LET YOUR READERS KNOW WHAT YOU'RE GOING TO DELIVER IN your post—in the very first sentence. That way, you're setting up expectations: And an expectation fulfilled is a satisfying post!

*Chapter Twenty-One*

# USE SHORT SENTENCES

EVEN IF YOU DECIDE A LONGER LENGTH IS PERFECT FOR A particular post, write in short, plain sentences. People's brains grow "tired", wading through compound sentences—especially with today's emphasis on mobile message protocols and instant gratification.

Cut out adjectives, adverbs and weakening (unnecessary) words or phrases. Read your post aloud. Say exactly what you want to say —no more; no less.

Facebook is all about connection. Use these tips to help your posts represent your brand in a way that truly connects.

# PART THREE

*Chapter Three*

# RESOURCE DIRECTORY

YOU DON'T HAVE TO WRACK YOUR BRAINS OVER EVERY Facebook post.

Take advantage of all the rich resources available to help you transform your posts into top-quality stories your fans will want to read.

Never has there been a better time to optimize your posts and deepen their emotional impact with all the tools available to help you with online content creation.

Start with even a handful of these twenty-one suggestion to generate better Facebook Post ideas and grow their emotional impact—and engagement!

*Chapter Twenty-Two*

# EASEL.LY

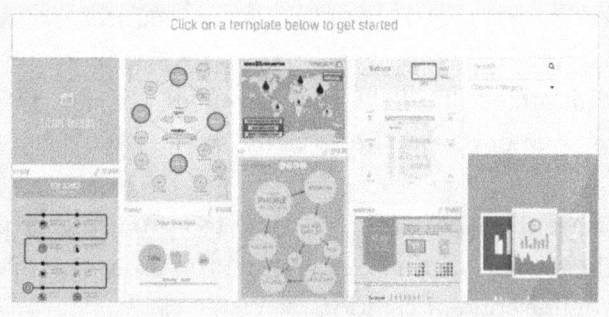

Theme-based web app that allows you to create infographics.

"Just drag a Theme onto your canvas," promised Easel.ly —as well as text, shapes, charts and other objects.

If you want to create an infographic quickly and easily, this is a simple way to do it—using pre-created, customizable, free templates for professional results.

*Chapter Twenty-Three*

# PIKTOCHART

ANOTHER TOP-QUALITY, WEB-BASED INFOGRAPHIC CREATION APP. (It's good to try out more than one, varying your content with different template styles—plus some web apps are better displaying one type of infographic, and others are better for displaying different types.)

Piktochart's library of 500 templates is updated weekly.

A particularly nice feature is the Online Presentation mode, which allows you to present your infographic anywhere like a slide show.

Also offers HTML or email options for you to download and embed your infographic, as well as the ability to download or print it in .JPG, .PNG and .PDF formats.

Piktochart offers a free lifetime account, and its paid plans start at $15.00 per month.

*Chapter Twenty-Four*

# CANVA

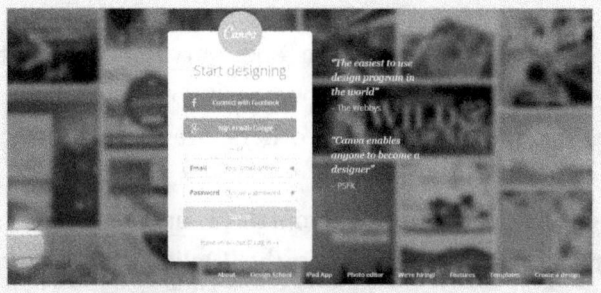

C anva is a rich online graphic design app that not only allows you to create infographics, but also images.

You can edit photos, log in with your email, Facebook or Google; and you can also use Canva as an iPad app.

Plus it offers some very cool photo effects and features not available on other graphic design apps.

You can also make postcards, presentations, banners, business cards and much more with Canva.

*Chapter Twenty-Five*

# INFOGR.AM

OFFERS FREE AND PAID ACCOUNTS.

The free plan allows you to create up to 10 infographics, 10 uploaded images, no private sharing and no downloads or live connections and their business account starts at $15.00 per month, billed annually.

*Chapter Twenty-Six*

# YOUZIGN

SIMILAR TO CANVA.

Also allows you to create YouTube Channel Art, Facebook Covers, Twitter covers and Twitter backgrounds.

Offers over 800 templates and "instant access to over one copyright-free million images from Pixabay, Iconfinder and StockUnlimited inside Youzign."

*Chapter Twenty-Seven*

# GIMP.ORG

FREE, OPEN-SOURCE IMAGE EDITOR.

Your best alternative to Adobe Photoshop.

Contains thorough tutorials, and has been in business for twenty years.

*Chapter Twenty-Eight*

# DEPOSITPHOTOS

Top-quality stock photo site that also provides HD video, illustrations and vector graphics, as well as editorial and news images.

Tends not to contain the same photos as other well-known stock photo sites—and a helpful feature is its "undiscovered" section, which allows you to know you are seeing truly original graphics that have not yet been used.

Offers a variety of pricing options, including monthly and daily credits—but keep your eyes peeled for their occasional promotions, which usually offer 1,000 photos with lifetime access for incredibly low prices.

If you see such an offer—grab it!

*Chapter Twenty-Nine*

## PIXABAY.COM

A FAVORITE, TOP-QUALITY FREE GRAPHICS SITE THAT OFFERS OVER 530,000 free photos, vectors and art illustrations.

Free for commercial use.

(Always check licensing information for each photo you use from free image sites.)

*Chapter Thirty*

# STORIFY

CONTENT CURATION SITE.

You don't have to write every single post yourself, you can simply share something fascinating, entertaining or important to your ideal fan.

A crucial part of content curating, however, lies in putting your own spin on whatever you are sharing, so be sure to at least introduce what you're sharing—or ask an irresistible question—or give your opinion and invite comments.

If you use Twitter, be aware that Storify is "Twitter Certified" and integrates flawlessly with this social platform. You can sign up for free, but if you plan to make content curation a significant part of your posting, consider Storify's "Enterprise" plan.

*Chapter Thirty-One*

# VISUAL.LY

I f you have a healthy budget and you'd like to outsource all your content creation, it's vital to select someone who thoroughly understands marketing, your business and social media.

If you have a healthy budget to set aside for this, Visual.ly should be one of the first companies that you checkout.

*Chapter Thirty-Two*

# HOOTSUITE

Online social media management app that allows you to pre-schedule and publish posts to multiple social media platforms.

You can log in with Twitter, Google or Facebook.

Includes powerful analytics options that allow you to track "engagement and conversions with insights from Twitter, Facebook, LinkedIn, Google+, and Google Analytics".

You can also use Hootsuite Campaigns to create and track effective social contests and campaigns.

# Chapter Thirty-Three

# CROWDBOOSTER

ALLOWS YOU TO FIND YOUR MOST ENGAGED FANS AND followers, schedule unlimited tweets "for optimal times" and measure your social analytics on a variety of platforms.

Plans start at $9.00 per month.

*Chapter Thirty-Four*

# PUBLIC DOMAIN IMAGES: WHAT IS ALLOWED AND WHAT IS NOT

EXCELLENT ARTICLE FROM THE PIXABAY BLOG ON THE CORRECT way to use public domain images.

https://pixabay.com/en/blog/posts/public-domain-images-what-is-allowed-and-what-is-4/

# Chapter Thirty-Five

# TAILWIND

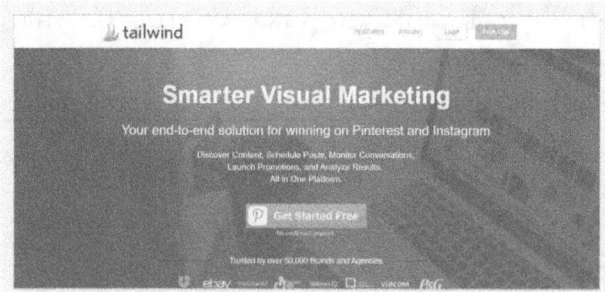

This top level Pinterest and Instagram content management app is unusual in that it provides a plan aimed at single bloggers (e.g. coaches)—which many of the apps catering to large business needs don't do.

As the screenshot says, you can "discover content, schedule posts, monitor conversations, launch promotions and analyze results"—all from the Tailwind platform... starting at only $9.99 per month.

*Chapter Thirty-Six*

# COSCHEDULE HEADLINE ANALYZER

CoSchedule is a great app site to help you with content creation and scheduling—and their customer service is superb—but this particular little free tool they provide is really handy for learning to create better headlines... instantly.

Simply enter your headline, let the tool analyze it—and try new versions. The app scores each headline and gives you constructive feedback, like this:

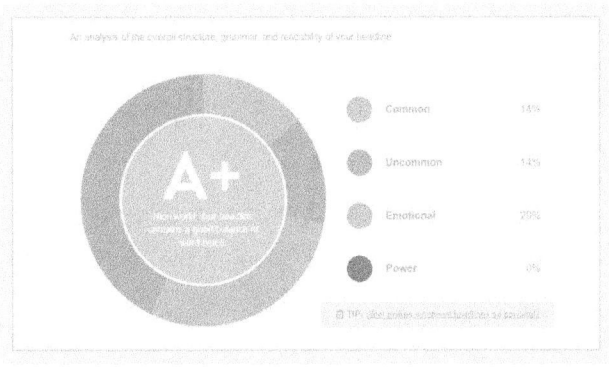

# Chapter Thirty-Seven

# FAQ FOX AND COSCHEDULE 1. FAQ FOX

## AQ Fox

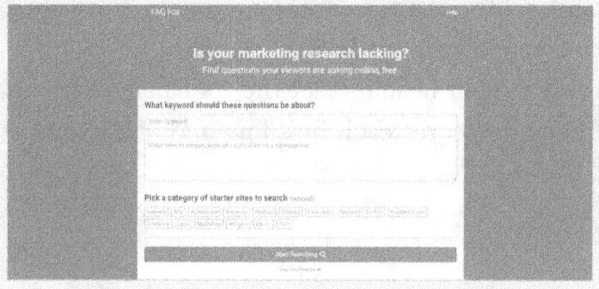

This handy, free app will help you come up with great content ideas—on topics your ideal fans actually care about. Here's how to use FAQ Fox most effectively:

- Enter a keyword you know your audience likes
- Enter the URL of one large, respected content site.

When you press "Start Searching", you'll be served up a list of relevant articles from that site

- Look for a new, relevant topic that jumps out at you within the list of articles

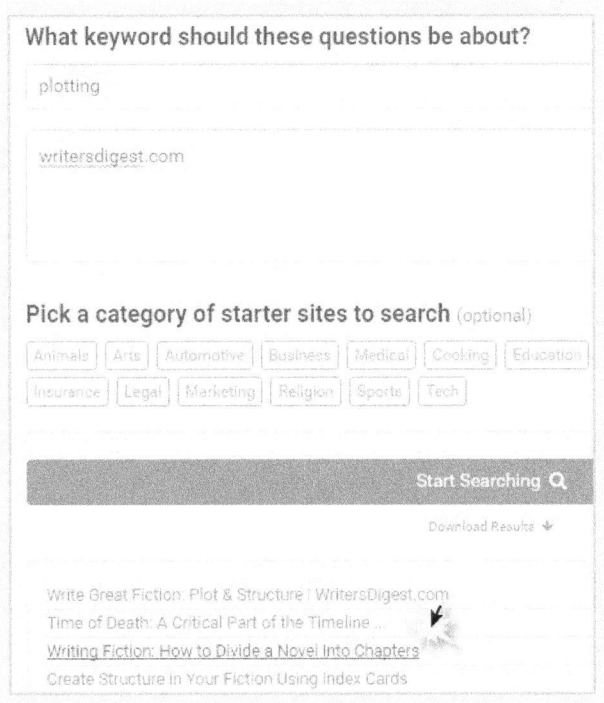

- Read that article—and see if one sentence or comment in it sparks an idea for a new article that incites your enthusiasm.

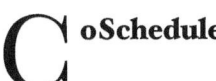 **oSchedule**

C oSchedule is a service, a suite of tools; but most of all, it is a great editorial calendar. You do have to pay—a "Solo" Calendar is $15.00 per month—but there is a free trial and lots of personalized support, if you need it.

Whether you invest in CoSchedule financially or not, keep up with their blog: Sign up, and get access to eighty invaluable free resources, like this post planning checklist:

# Chapter Thirty-Eight

# AMINSTITUTE HEADLINE ANALYZER

ANOTHER QUICK, FREE, EFFECTIVE HEADLINE ANALYZER THAT HAS been going for years.

Helps you determine, among other things, the emotional impact of your headlines.

*Chapter Thirty-Nine*

# GIPHY FOR CHROME

INSTALL THIS APP TO QUICKLY FIND ANIMATED .GIFs FOR YOUR posts. And if you don't want to do that, simply search directly, with either keywords or hashtags by running a Giphy search.

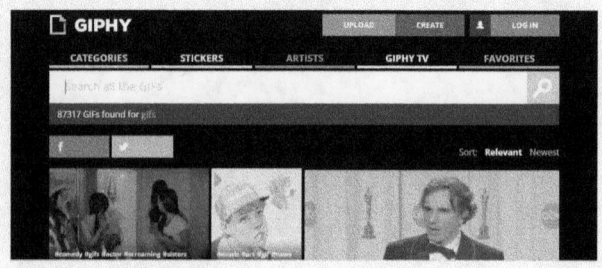

*Chapter Forty*

# EVERNOTE

THERE ARE MORE THAN ONE REASONS CONTENT WRITERS everywhere love Evernote:

- You can quickly jot down post ideas, no matter where you are
- It syncs in real-time between all your devices
- You can use it to create To-Do lists
- You can keep research links and results handy

And its basic plan is free.

*Chapter Forty-One*

# WORDCOUNTER

LIKE TO WRITE YOUR POSTS IN TEXT EDITORS OTHER THAN MS Word?

Just visit WordCounter and copy paste your post into the text field box, to instantly generate an accurate word count.

# ABOUT THE AUTHOR

**Alun Hill** is the millionaire owner of 32 businesses.

He lives with his wife on a tiny island in the Mediterranean Sea.

A long time international TV and Radio journalist and broadcaster, he has spent his working life reporting from most corners of the planet.

He still travels the world almost continuously, both speaking to business audiences and listening to business owners.

In each case, he learns about business problems and solutions and shows ways of improving these business models.

*He has now taught almost 100,000 people, all over the world (both in person and via his online courses), the skills to succeed in their own, usually home based, business.*

His 50 page monthly newsletter has many thousands of subscribers and is available for free from

http://alunhill.com

Importantly, it never contains any adverts, affiliate links or sales items.

This is very important to Alun, who strives to produce content that is solely of genuine interest to those looking to ....

**"make an extra $1,000 a month"**

~

**http://AlunHill.com**

www.ingramcontent.com/pod-product-compliance
Lightning Source LLC
Chambersburg PA
CBHW071250170526
45165CB00003B/1290

* 9 781548 500672 *